PRIVATE LESSONS

GUITAR BASICS
LEVEL 1

by Bruce Buckingham

"This book is dedicated to my wife, Kim, the love of my life"

ISBN 0-7935-7131-6

7777 W. BLUEMOUND RD. P.O. BOX 13819 MILWAUKEE, WI 53213

Visit Hal Leonard Online at
www.halleonard.com

About the Author

Bruce has been a professional musician and music teacher for over 25 years. He joined the staff at G.I.T. in 1980, and has since taught guitar to thousands of students from around the world. Bruce plays guitar in many styles, but specializes in jazz, Latin, blues, and funk. He has played and/or recorded with a numnber of diverse and notable musicians, including Helen Reddy, John Patitucci, and Michael Jackson. Bruce divides his time between live gigs, studio work, and teaching at M.I. in Hollywood, California. He is currently working on his own recording project and continues to develop additional instructional products for M.I. Press.

Bruce can be reached by fax at (310) 399-0137, or online at BruceBuckingham@Compuserve.com.

Bruce Buckingham

Table of Contents

About the CD

The accompanying CD provides a practice tool that includes full-band backing for each of the examples in this book. The diamond audio icons (◆1) correspond with the CD track numbers. Use track 1 to tune.

Each track begins with one measure played by the drums. Listen closely to these "pickup" measures in order to accurately adjust to the tempo and eighth-note feel (straight or shuffle). Count 1, 2, 3, 4; 1, 2, 3, 4; then join the band at a volume slightly below the volume of the CD. Use the CD to memorize all the chords, stimulate your own rhythms, and to practice "locking in" with a rhythm section.

Preface

Most guitarists spend several years floundering around the guitar until finally something clicks and they see some logic to the way the neck is laid out (and some never do see it). This is due primarily to the lack of a clear and concise introduction to the basics.

It is my purpose to present beginning through advanced studies emphasizing the fundamentals—chords, scales, improvisation, and basic theory. This will enable the student to build a strong foundation of fretboard knowledge, technique, and musical awareness.

Having taught at Musicians Institute for 17 years and written curriculum for a wide variety of subjects at different levels of ability, it has become apparent that the most progress is made by the student who is sufficiently self-motivated and has a clear course of study. A student that practices on a regular basis can mark progress by how relaxed they play and how well they "see" the neck (this "seeing" also exists in the mind's eye). In this book then, are the most practical chord voicings, scale shapes, chord progressions, and rhythm patterns. I would ask you to master each example and review them often. Memorize each example as you are practicing it; listen to and play along with the CD to get the rhythmic feel and dynamics (loud, soft).

Again, the purpose is to present essential information—the kind of things that every guitarist can play. As a result, we can learn a vocabulary that is essential to all guitar styles.

Good luck with the book and keep practicing!

Bruce Buckingham

Chapter One

1 CHORDS IN OPEN POSITION

The beginner moves to advanced primarily through his or her understanding of *chords;* both their structure on the instrument and in music theory.

Phase 1	Phase 2
The first steps for guitarists can be outlined as...	The next steps explore the neck through a variety of systems that each share insight to the inner workings of the fretboard. Some might be...

Phase 1
1. Open position (essential chords)
2. Moveable chord forms (barre chords)
3. Strumming
4. Progressions
5. Repertoire (memorized songs)

Phase 2
1. Inversions
2. Power chords
3. Substitution
4. Chordal Embellishment
5. String combinations
6. Arpeggios

You've probably heard most of these terms before and you may understand a few of them. It is not the intention of this book to introduce all of these subjects, but rather to give you the basic chords and scales and talk about their application. How many chords you learn and how quickly you learn them is based on practice habits and time itself. More important is what you do with the chords and scales you *can* play!

We'll start by learning an area of the guitar called *open position.* Here we'll play 21 chords that are the most practical and best-sounding in this position. But first let's learn how to interpret the typical guitar diagram.

The Diagram

The vertical diagram pictures a five-fret area and is used to show where and how to play notes and chords on the guitar.

The *frets* are the wires, however the "fret area" (the space between one fret and the next) is generally referred to as the "fret." Frets are numbered from the lowest (#1) all the way up the neck (toward the guitar's "body") to the highest. The *strings* are also numbered. The highest pitched string is string 1 and the lowest pitched string is string 6. The note pictured in Fig. 1 is the "third string, fourth fret." Finally, your left-hand fingers are numbered 1-4 as in Fig. 2

Fig. 1

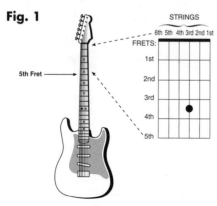

Fig. 2

Fig. 3

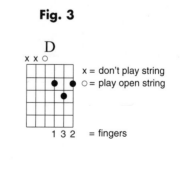

x = don't play string
○ = play open string

= fingers

☞ Fret numbers (e.g. "5fr") may appear to the right of the first fret on some diagrams to indicate a different starting fret other than fret 1.

Open Position Major Chords

The first 21 chords we'll learn are *major, minor,* and *dominant* chord types built from the seven natural root notes (A-B-C-D-E-F-G). These are termed "natural" since their letter names are not used in combination with a sharp (♯) or flat (♭). The letter is also called the root. The root gives the chord its name and also functions as the first note in the respective chord's scale.

Memorize each chord with its correct name. Learn to interpret the diagram and utilize the fingerings given. Try other fingerings that seem reasonable and find your personal preference.

Major

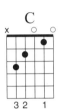    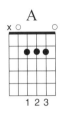  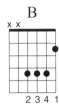

Dominant 7th

 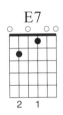   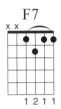 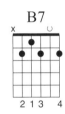

Minor

     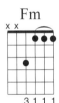 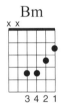

NOTE: The chords above are the most common and practical chord shapes in open position. Chords that have sharps or flats in the root (e.g. A♭m) are best dealt with as "barre" or "moveable" chord forms.

1

Chord Pairs

Once you're comfortable fingering chords, try using them in combinations. As you practice switching between the two-chord examples in this lesson, observe the following:

Getting a Smooth Connection

As you switch from chord to chord, determine the common tones (if any) within each fingering. If one or two fingers remain on the same note, allow them to stay pressed as you change chords.

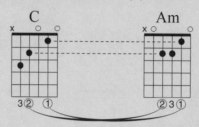

Troubleshooting the Fretting Hand

Most obvious flaws can be attributed to one of the following problems:

1. Missed note

   SOLUTION: Be sure to strum through all the notes in the chord.

2. Wrong placement of your finger in the fret

   SOLUTION: Always place your finger in the middle of the fret, or towards the front part just behind the next fret.

3. Part of one finger is blocking another (or two fingers on the same string)

   SOLUTION: Arch your fingers more by bringing your wrist further under the fingerboard.

4. String(s) not pressed down hard enough.

   SOLUTION: Use leverage from both your fingers and thumb to press down harder.

Practice playing the following chord pairs beginning with simple quarter-note strums (one strum per beat). Listen to the recording and try different rhythms as you become more comfortable. Use a metronome and practice daily!

Fig. 1 **2**

A
| D | A | D |

B
| C | G | C |

C
| E | D | E |

D
| A | E | A |

E
| Am | Dm | Am |

...More Chord Pairs

The importance of chord pair exercises cannot be over-emphasized. No matter how complex a chord progression is, it still breaks down to movements from one chord to the next. If you struggle playing full progressions or songs in the future, isolate the chord moves that are problematic and rehearse that change until you're able to play it well. However, practicing open chords as a daily ritual (at least 15 minutes) will eventually make the chords "second nature"(you'll instantly react when you see a chord symbol (C7) rather than having to think of each fingering and note placement.

Now try five more two-chord progressions:

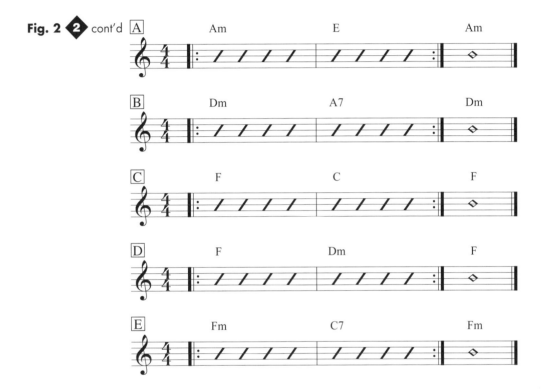

Practice Tips

- Play each chord pair as many times as possible in one practice session; pick up the next day where you left off. (The band on the CD only plays each pair four times due to time restraints.)

- Check the fretting hand regularly. If you hear a bad note, pluck through the chord one string at a time to find the troublesome string. Wiggle your fingers into place, don't muscle it.

- After a couple of weeks, try making up more pairs. Find some that sound good and some that sound a little unusual. This is the start of your composition and *improvisation* skills.

- Work on keeping the "time" steady. Relax and make music out of a simple exercise. Also, try varying the dynamics (loud and soft).

Perseverance and relaxation are your friends; laziness and frustration are the enemy!

Rhythm, Time, and Groove

Rhythm, time, and *groove* are the glue that holds the music together. The term "rhythm" refers to a song's steady pulse; it is the foundation that should be unshakable. "Time" refers to your rhythm as compared to a metronome. Staying accurate to the metronome translates to "good time," or in slang, "tight" to the beat. Finally, a "groove" happens when rhythmic patterns repeat. A "good groove" is created if the patterns compliment one another, offering a relaxed, in-the-pocket pattern.

To practice these elements, start by learning to play accurate quarter note rhythm using downstrokes in the strumming hand. In other words, attack the chords on each of the beats (1...2...3...4...is called a "downbeat"):

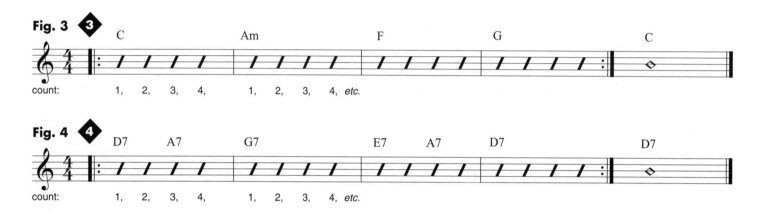

Next try eighth notes (two strums per beat). Be sure to keep your foot tapping on the downbeats.

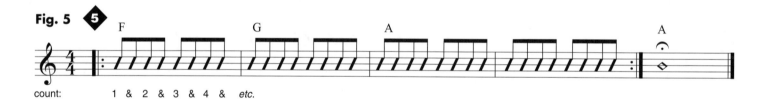

Now strum only the "upbeats," or the beats in between the downbeats. They occur on the "and" of the beat when your foot is all the way up. Practice this example over and over until you're able to keep accurate control over the chords even as you continue to tap your foot on the downbeats.

Figure 7 introduces a repeated figure, or groove. Use a downstroke for the first strum and an upstrum for the second. Then try two downstrokes—experiment.

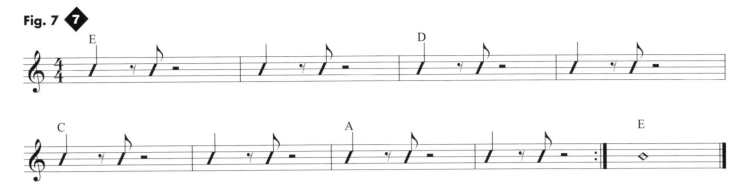

Now it's time to combine the elements you just learned into the following chord pairs. Listen along with the CD and then try strumming along. Start with simple rhythmic patterns and later progress to improvising some of your own. Above all, stay in the groove!

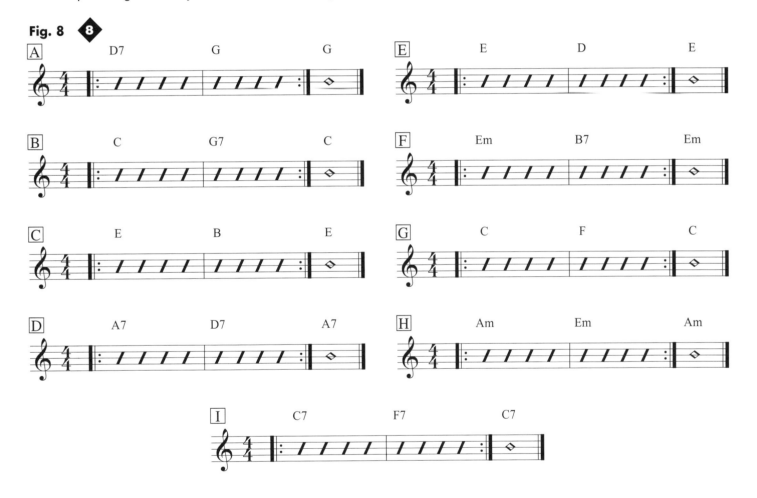

NOTE: In general, hash marks tell you to interpret the chords according to the style. For now, follow the duration assigned to each chord and strum along. When in doubt of the intended style, start with quarter-note strums.

Strumming

Good strumming technique involves a relaxed and even attack. If your strum is awkward, the music won't groove—so keep your foot tapping and your right hand in a constant down-up motion.

Practice the one-measure patterns below using one chord, then two chords, and finally a full chord progression.

Fig. 9

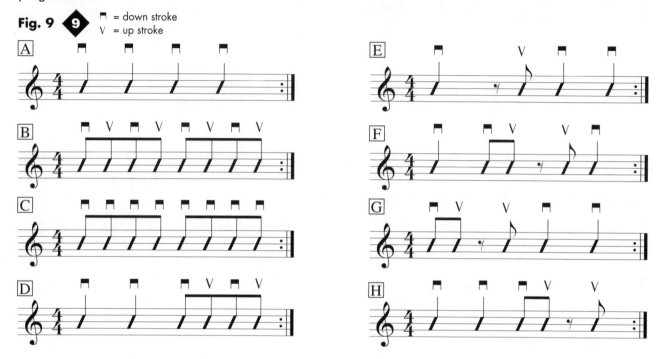

Now apply each of the patterns above to the following chord pairs. Afterward, begin to improvise your own strumming variations.

Fig. 10

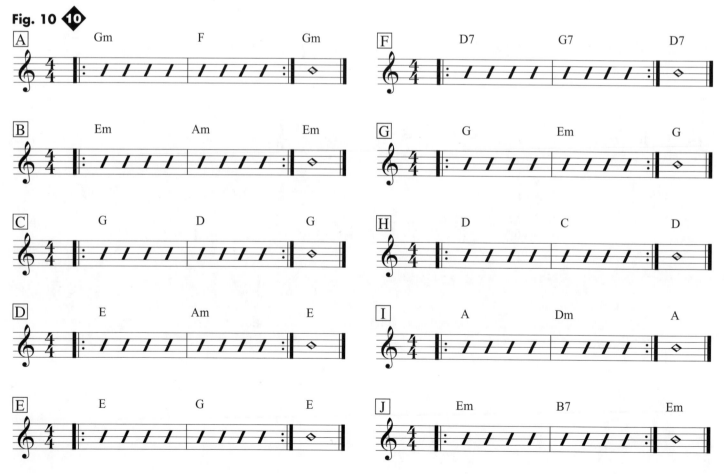

Getting in Rhythm

Rhythmically speaking, there are two different accompaniment "feels:"

1 The **straight** eighth-note feel uses regular even eighth notes using equal subdivision.

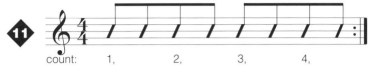

2 The **shuffle** or **swing** eighth-note feel is derived from a "triplet" feel, slicing the beat into three equal parts.

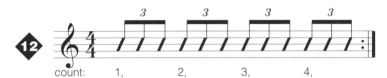

The actual shuffle or swing strum applies the triplet feel with the middle triplet omitted. The result is a very recognizable "long, short, long, short" sound that is especially prominent in blues music.

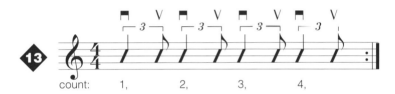

Play and memorize each of the patterns below. On the CD, both straight eighth and shuffle rhythms are demonstrated.

Fig. 11 **14**

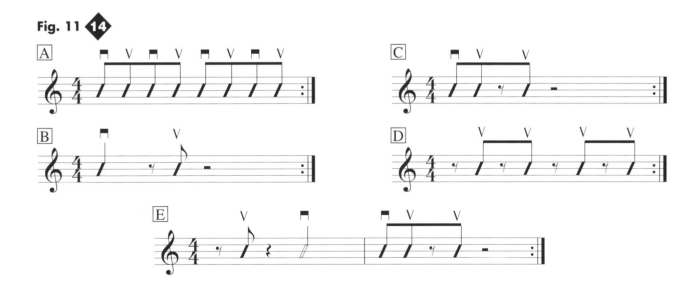

☞ DON'T FORGET: Try different tempos, always listen for the sub-division of the beat, strive for rhythmic accuracy, and relax!

Points to Remember

 Musical styles are often defined by the rhythmic feel or "sub-division" of the beat:

- Rock—straight eighths
- Blues—shuffle eighths
- Country—straight eighths (with an emphasis on the upbeat)
- Jazz—shuffle (or swing) eighths
- Reggae—shuffle eighths (with an emphasis on the upbeat)
- Ska—straight eighths
- Latin—straight eighths or sixteenths
- Funk—straight eighths or sixteenths
- R&B—straight and shuffle eighths or sixteenths
- Hiphop—shuffle sixteenths
- Pop—everything

Of course, this is a general statement about the style. There are blues tunes that use straight eighths, and rock tunes that use shuffle eighths.

 Be aware of the tempo (speed) and rhythmic style of the music you listen to.

 Practice improvising your strumming by changing the patterns, dynamics, and accents.

 Don't get bored with repetition. Repeat progressions many, many times to build your consistency, endurance, and rhythmic vocabulary.

 Write down all of the strum patterns you know; listen to records and make up some more.

Progressions for Practice

Chord progressions provide the *harmony* for songs. Play the examples on the next page along with the CD; then practice them alone and carry the groove all by yourself. Again, repetition will build strength and stamina in your fretting hand.

Notice the number of beats per chord varies—everything is not four beats per chord. This is referred to as a progression's *harmonic rhythm*.

Fig. 12

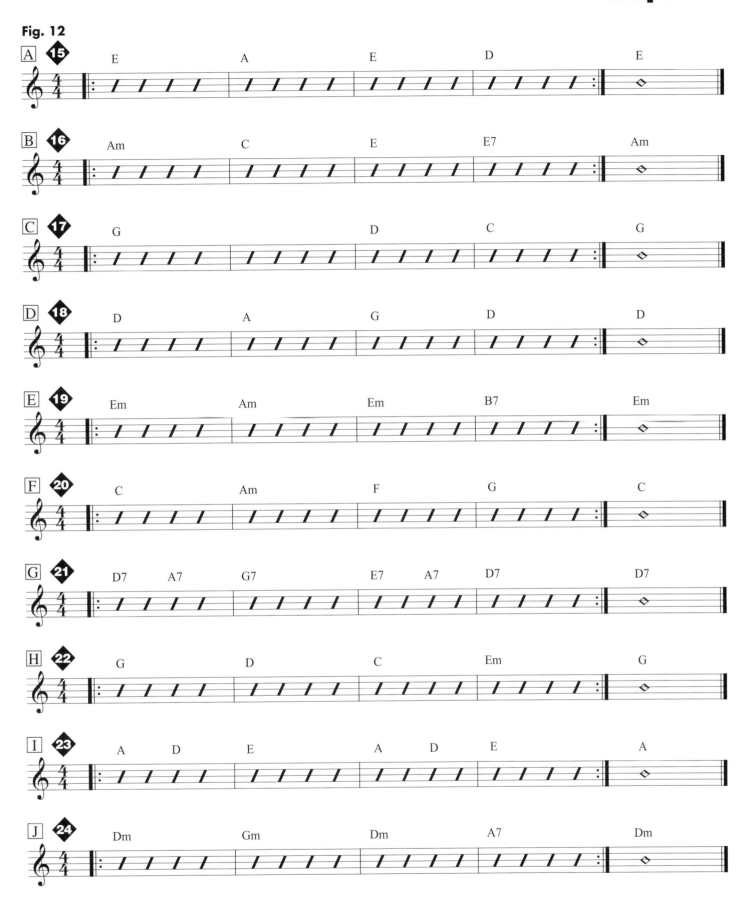

Tunes

Figs. 13-15 are 16-measure progressions. Play them as a song using the suggested accompaniment strums. Listen to the CD to hear how style and dynamics are implied with the guitar, bass, and drums together.

SAMPLE SONG #1

This is a straight ahead pop tune in 4/4 time.

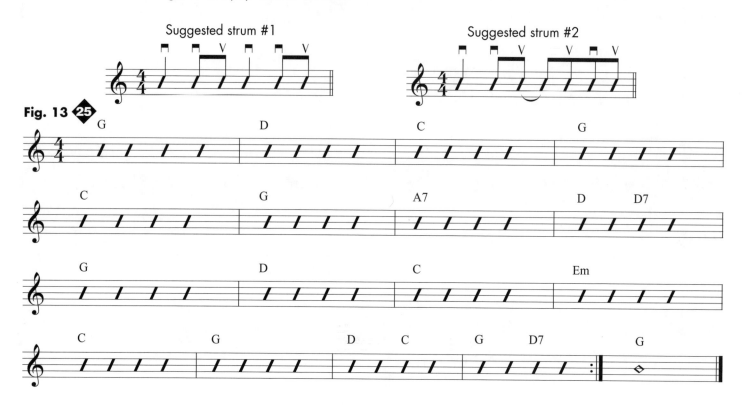

SAMPLE SONG #2

The next example is in 3/4 time—that means there are three beats per measure.

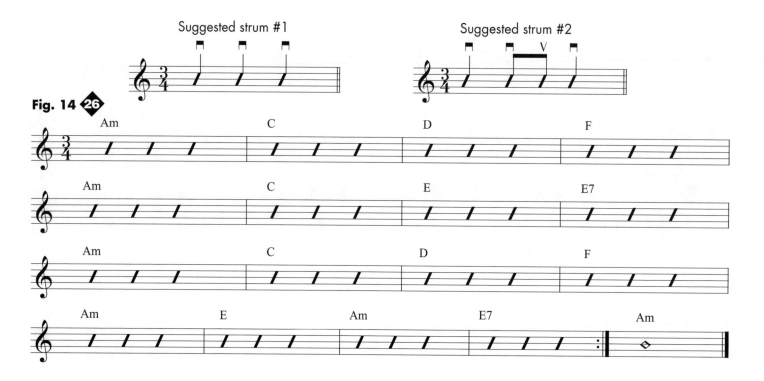

SAMPLE SONG #3

This tune features a reggae-type feel using eighth-note shuffle strums on the second and fourth beats of each measure. Follow the rhythm indicated in the first measure, then continue in a like manner (simile) for the remainder of the song. Mute the strings so there is silence with your strumming hand on beats 1 and 3.

Fig. 15

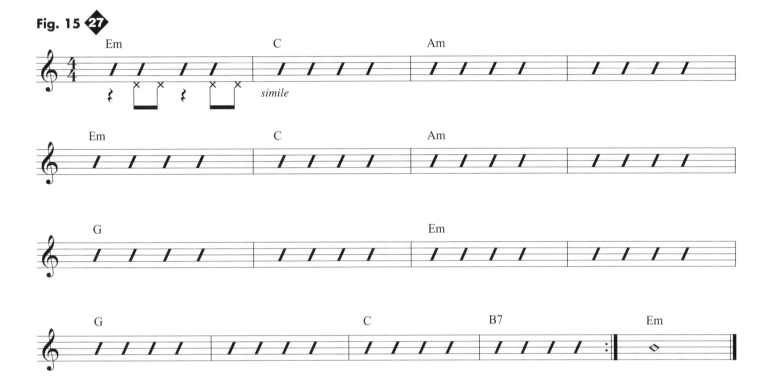

Chapter Two

2 SCALES IN OPEN POSITION

Learning the names of the notes on the fretboard is essential for all players. To begin, let's review the seven letters of the musical alphabet: A-B-C-D-E-F-G. As you learned in Chapter 1, these notes are referred to as natural since they do not contain a sharp (♯) or flat (♭). Chromatic notes are located between the natural notes and may be written using a sharp or flat. For example, the note between A and B can be named either A♯ or B♭. However, a chromatic note does not appear between the notes B and C, or E and F. As a result, there are twelve different notes (or pitches) in music. Observe the diagram below:

Fig. 1

$$A \underset{B\flat}{\overset{A\sharp}{+}} B - C \underset{D\flat}{\overset{C\sharp}{+}} D \underset{E\flat}{\overset{D\sharp}{+}} E - F \underset{G\flat}{\overset{F\sharp}{+}} G \underset{A\flat}{\overset{G\sharp}{+}} A$$

This is also visually displayed on the piano. The white keys are the natural notes and the black keys are the chromatic notes:

Fig. 2

A B C D E F G A

Scale Shapes

In open position, the natural notes give us the shape and pitches for the key of C major. Memorize the general pattern, the root (tonic), and fingering, as well as the individual notes themselves.

note names

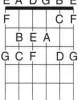

C major

- circled note is the tonic or root (1st note of the major scale)

- numbers represent finger and fret numbers

scale shape

Picking

Practice scales using quarter notes with a downpick motion. That is, the pick strikes the string with a downward motion. Once the scale is memorized, alternate using a downpick for the first note and an uppick for the second. This is referred to as alternate picking.

Different Keys

Different keys require the use of sharps or flats. To play in the key of G major, raise F to F♯:

G major

note names

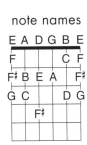

scale shape

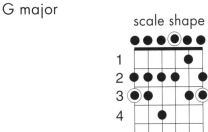

The key of D major retains the F♯ from G major and adds one new one (C♯).

A major retains the two sharps from D major and adds one more of its own (G♯).

D major

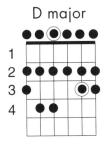

A major

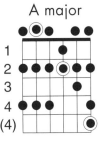

Practicing Scales

Practice these four scales daily in order to:

- Memorize the notes on the fretboard.
- Learn the shape for each key.
- Develop coordination between the picking and fretting hands.
- Observe the theory (which sharps are added).
- Gain control over quarter notes and eighth notes by using a metronome.

Sixteenth Notes

Sixteenth notes further sub-divide the beat into four parts. They are twice as fast as (or double) the pulse of an eighth note.

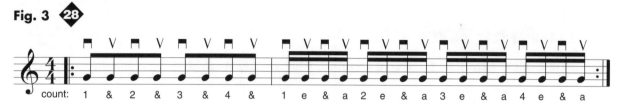

The following patterns and exercises are designed to get you familiar with various sixteenth note rhythms, and help you increase your coordination and picking skills. You don't need to read music—just use one note, follow the patterns and picking directions, and use the CD to help you memorize the sound by ear. Then practice the patterns at various tempos. Start slow and even! After this become comfortable, practice the rhythms along with the scales learned earlier. Play the scales up and back using alternate picking. Repeat as many times as possible.

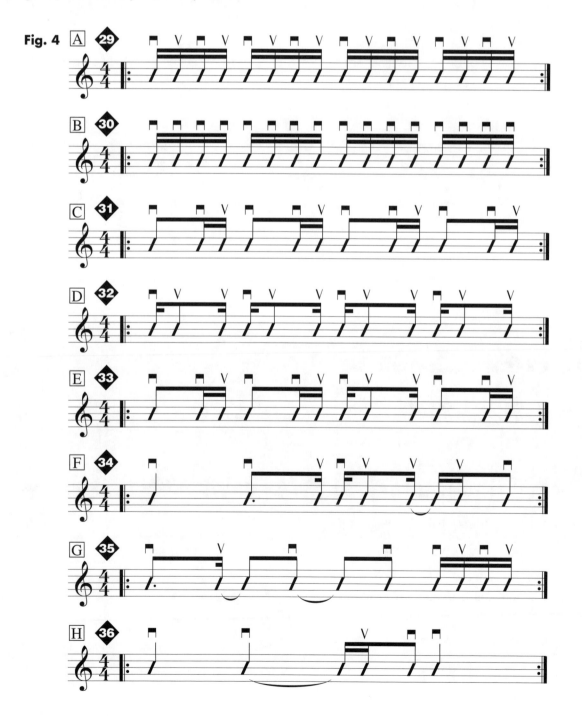

Now use sixteenth rhythms as strumming exercises. Play the rhythms below using different chord progressions and tempos. (The CD demonstrates the rhythms using an E chord only.)

You've been exposed to many rhythms so far. However, "good rhythm" can only be achieved through constant repetition. As you progress through the rest of this book, review the basic rhythm patterns often and try to incorporate them into the chord pairs and songs you may be working on. Also, be creative and write some progressions of your own. Remember, rhythm is all around you in the music you listen to. Copy it, repeat it, and use it!

Chapter Three

3

PRACTICE TIPS

It is difficult for students to stay on top of all the information and technique without some method of practice and regular review. Unfortunately, most players tend not to develop good practice habits until they become more advanced (if they get that far). Players who develop good practice skills from the beginning progress much more rapidly.

Below are five important keys to making your practice sessions a success.

1. **Learn new material**: Repetition is important. However, too much repetition can lead to boredom. Avoid practicing old ideas you can already play without any problem. The key is to know when to let something go and when to stimulate your learning process with new material.

2. **Vary your practice topics**: Strive for steady progress in all areas of your playing. Spend time working on physical skills (technique drills, scales, picking exercises), chords, theory, and repertoire (songs, licks, riffs, etc.).

3. **Review**: Regular review must be quick and easy. It is important to look back and make sure you've retained earlier concepts, but don't allow the review process to extend further than it needs to. Organize your goals and see to it that you follow them.

4. **Spontaneous Ideas**: Capitalize on new ideas that pop out when you're playing. Write them down, extend them further, and work them into your own "style."

5. **Have Fun**: Always make sure you're having fun. Go ahead and learn a few of your favorite songs or set aside time for your own private "jam session."

Practice Space

In order to accomplish your goals as a guitarist set aside a practice area that is all music (ideally all your own). That is, the space cannot double as the TV room, bedroom, or place where others work. Have the right tools and keep them set up all the time, ready to go. Your time is valuable, so get the most out of it!

Here are the tools you should have in your practice space:

- Good music stand
- Good chair
- Good lighting
- Paper, pencil, and eraser
- Metronome (eventually a drum machine and/or sequencer)
- Tape deck (eventually a 4- or 8-track)
- Quiet!

Loosen up physically with stretching and divide your rehearsal time between standing and sitting. This helps out your back (sitting) and at the same time simulates a performance setting (standing).

Short Practice Sessions

Short time frames of 10 to 30 minutes are ideal. If you switch subjects every 10 to 30 minutes, you'll will keep a fresh ear and outlook. Stand up between subjects and stretch, walk around, or maybe find something to drink. In the long run, short sessions will be more efficient and less boring.

Below is a sample practice schedule for a session that extends about an hour and 15 minutes. Of course, your personal routine can and will change according to the your job and social schedules, but the fact remains the more you practice the faster you will gain skills. As a result, be aware of your own time management and make practicing the guitar a priority.

Sample Practice Schedule

 2 minutes Warm up playing open strings

- with the pick using alternate strokes (down and up)
- with just the thumb (all downstrokes)
- with the thumb and first finger alternating

 10 minutes Play each chord individually to determine which are memorized and which need work. Make a list and keep track of it. It is very important to know every chord presented so far and feel comfortable playing them.

 15 minutes Work on chord pairs.

SHORT BREAK

 15 minutes Work on writing your own progressions. Write them down so you can keep track.

 15 minutes Listen to music and try to analyze what you hear! Eventually you should be playing along even if it is just on one string or a bass motion.

SHORT BREAK

 **15 minutes** Work on memorizing and practicing scales.

- all downstrokes (slow and steady)
- all upstrokes
- alternate downstrokes and upstrokes

Other Projects:

Keep a music journal with thoughts and observations about:

- what you are practicing
- your strengths and weaknesses
- tempos for practicing progressions and scales
- other observations concerning your practicing and music in general

Chapter Four

MOVEABLE CHORDS AND SCALES

Moveable chord forms, or *barre chords* allow you to transfer a common shape up and down the neck. The location of the shape's root note on the neck determines the chord's letter name. To start, practice barring your first finger across all six strings:

Now try adding other fingers for your first three barre shapes.

  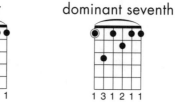

As we discussed earlier, the *root* of a chord is the note that names the chord. In the shapes above, the root is located on the sixth, or lowest string. Use the fretboard diagram below to help you memorize the notes on the sixth string.

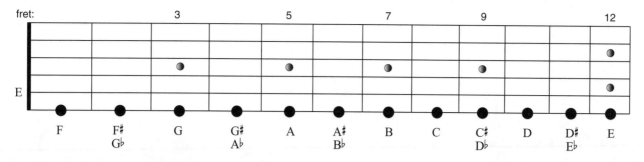

Naming Barre Chords

If the major barre chord shape above is played beginning at the fifth fret, it would be an A major chord [Fig. 1]. A chord at the third fret using the minor shape would be Gm [Fig. 2], and a dominant seventh shape at the first fret would be F7 [Fig. 3].

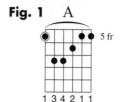  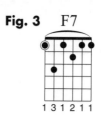

DON'T GIVE UP: Barre chords take a couple of weeks to get the hang of. Practice in short spurts and take breaks often to let your hand rest. Listen to the sound you are projecting from the instrument. Are each of the notes ringing out clearly? Perseverance is the key and repetition is the teacher.

Moveable Chords with Fifth-String Roots

Memorize the shapes and fifth-string roots below:

major   minor   dominant seventh

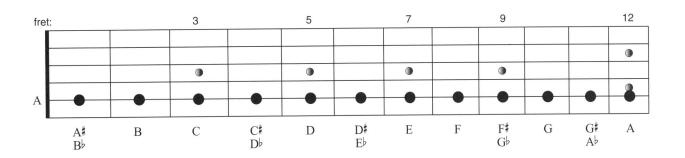

Now look at the chart below. Make sure you understand how and why each chord is labeled as it is. Then test yourself and make a practice exercise out of naming barre chords as quickly as possible. You can start by playing a chord and trying to name it, or thinking of a chord name and trying to locate it.

Chord	Root String	Root Fret	Diagram
Fm	6	1	Fm
Gm	6	3	Gm
C7	6 or 5	8 or 3	C7 (8 fr) / C7
B♭	6 or 5	6 or 1	B♭ (6 fr) / B♭

4

Two-Chord Progressions

Practice making the connection between two barre chord shapes in the progressions below. Look at the roots and say the name of each chord as you move from one to the next. Start with quarter-note strums (all downstrokes) and move to eighth-notes when the switching becomes more smooth. Then play along with the CD and improvise your strums with the groove. Daily practice will smooth out the chord transitions, and playing with a metronome will keep your "time" awareness sharp.

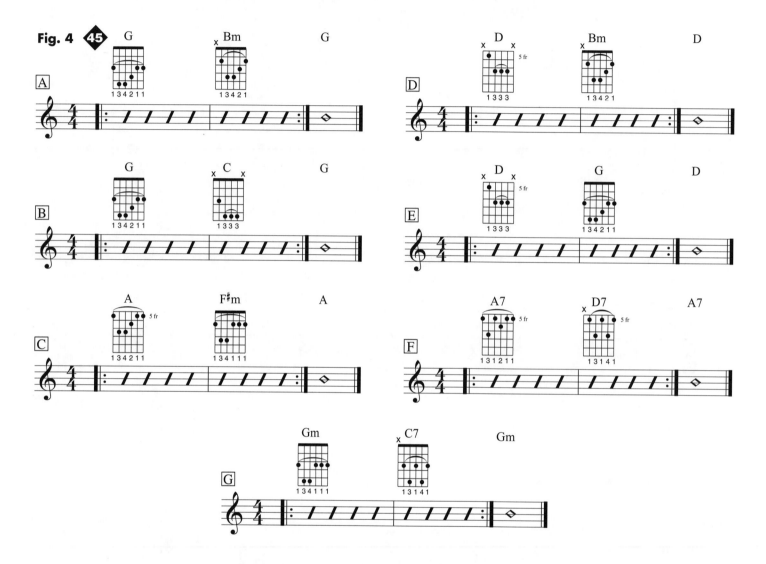

Four-Measure Progressions

Now try some longer progressions using barre chords. Follow the information below the staff telling which string the root in on. Relax and concentrate on accuracy. Remember, barre chords are essential to guitar playing and one of the first major obstacles to get over. Keep practicing!

Fig. 5

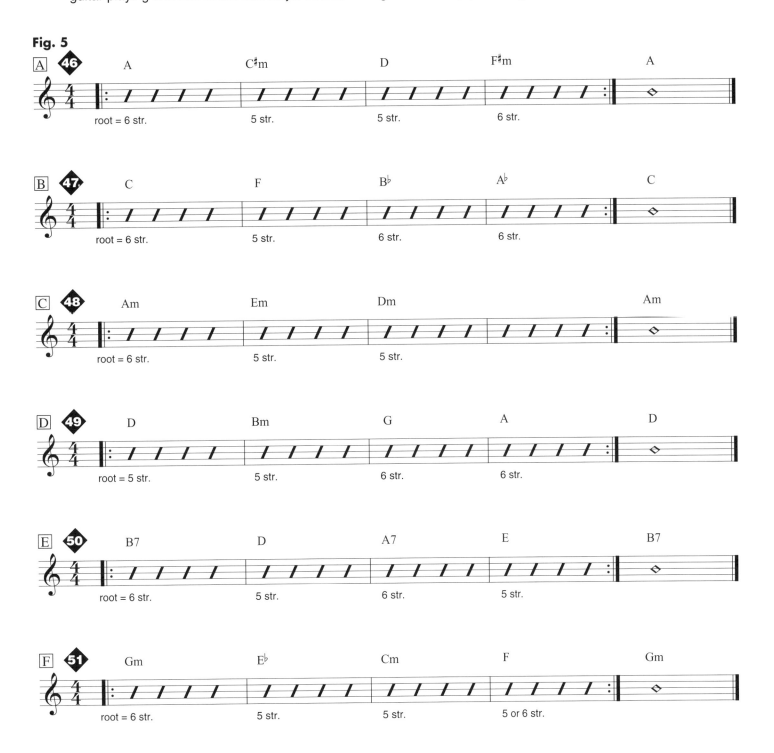

Moveable Chord Exercise

Use the following guidelines to practice the sample song below.

• Play using only moveable chords with sixth-string roots

• Play using only moveable chords with fifth-string roots

• Combine both string choices to economize your hand motion

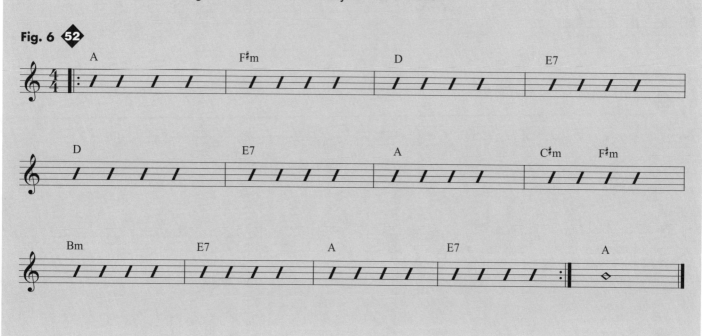

Writing Your Own Progressions

You're now ready to begin composing your own progressions. Simply make up any combination of chords and play. Don't worry if they are "correct", just listen—if the chords sound good to you, then play 'em. As you learn more songs and understand more theory, you can put more thought into what you want to do. For now, anything goes. Few things improve your musical skills more than writing.

You can also create progressions that attack your strengths and weaknesses. Use chords that fall naturally under your fingers, and combine them with one or two that seem awkward. Eventually all the chord shapes will feel comfortable.

Power Chords

Power chords are two-note chords built from the root and fifth of the scale. Commonly used with distortion, they offer a unique texture that has become the standard tone for most rock and blues guitarists.

Below are two common power chord voicings.

Now try playing the four-measure progressions below. Use a clean sound at first and then try a distorted tone. Attack the strings using all downstrokes in a steady eighth-note groove. Mute the unwanted strings with the remaining fingers on your fretting hand. Also note that the written chord symbols use the number 5 after the letter (root) name.

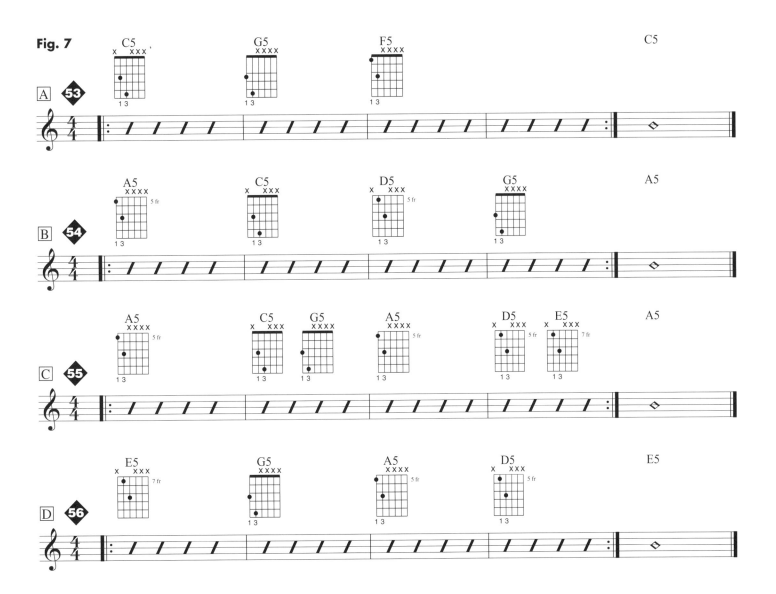

Boogie Bass Patterns

Below are two variations of the power chord shape. The first adds the pinkie two frets above the fifth; the second adds the pinkie three frets above the fifth. Practice alternating these shapes with the basic power chord shapes learned earlier. Use all downstrokes and listen closely to the resulting distinctive rock 'n' roll boogie sound.

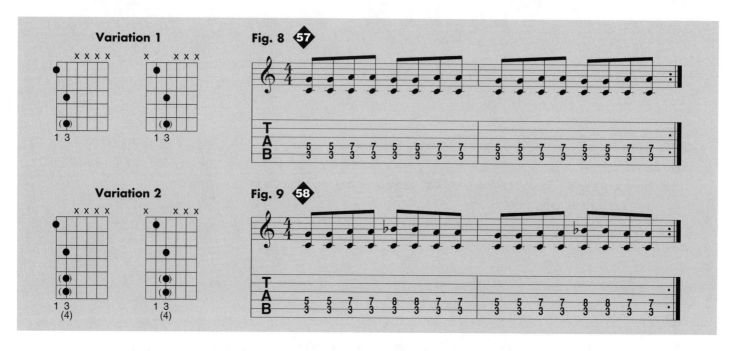

More Practice Progressions

Now incorporate these boogie variations into the following progressions. Also try each of the examples using different root locations. In other words, play C5 at the third fret (fifth-string root) and at the eighth fret (sixth-string root).

Fig. 10

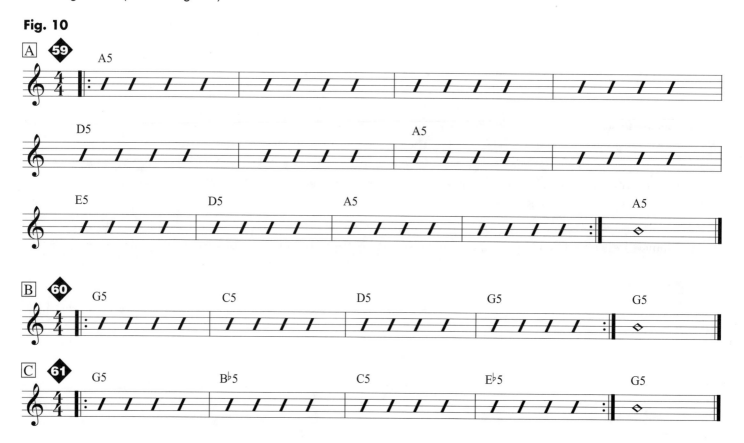

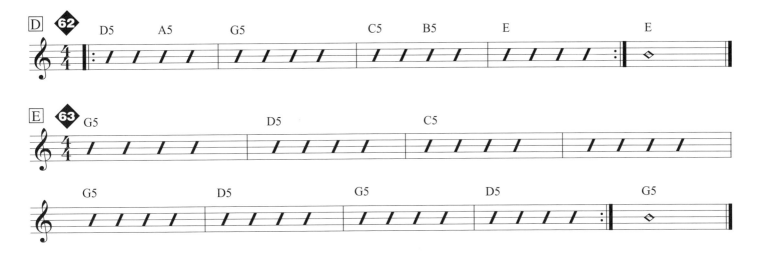

Moveable Pentatonic Scales

As their name suggests ("penta" means five), pentatonic scales contain only five different tones. They are commonly used in nearly all styles of music, especially rock and blues. Memorize the shapes below and practice playing them using alternate picking. Since there are only two-notes-per-string, pentatonic scales are perfect for developing your technique (first down, second up). Like moveable chords, moveable scales are named by their root, or tonic.

Continue practicing at a steady and even pace at least fifteen minutes a day. Use a metronome, relax your fingers, and make sure you stay on the tips of your fingers.

Keys

Use the major pentatonic scale when you're in a major key, and the minor pentatonic scale when you're in a minor key. However, sometimes the minor pentatonic works better in major-based blues and rock tunes. Use your ear and switch to what sounds best.

Although soloing (lead guitar) goes beyond the scope of this book, jamming on these scales will immediately benefit your technique and ears. Turn on the radio and try improvising along using one of the moveable scales above. Think rhythm and tap your foot.

Chapter Five
THE BLUES

5

The Blues Form

The most common blues form extends twelve measures and is referred to as the *twelve-bar blues*. It continues to have a profound impact on rock, jazz, country, pop, and of course, blues music throughout the world.

Let's take a look at what this progression consists of. First of all, there are three main chords:

- The "one" chord, or I. (In the key of A, the A chord.)

- The "four" chord, or IV. (In the key of A, the D chord.)

- The "five" chord, or V. (In the key of A, the E chord.)

Now that we have the basic chords, we can take a look at the progression itself. The example below is a twelve-bar blues in the key of A.

Fig. 1

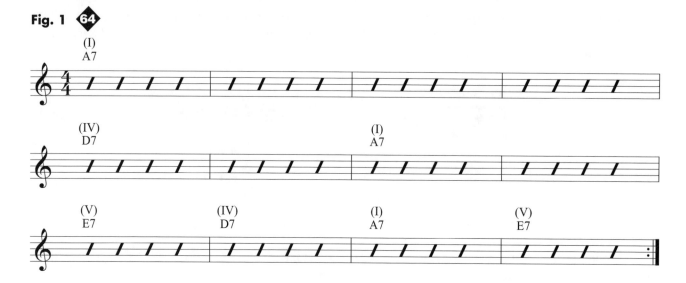

Memorize the Form

Commit the order of chords in the twelve-bar blues to memory. You'll recognize there are three, four-bar phrases. Listen as you play along and memorize the sound as well. Try different tempos and feels—learn to immediately know where you are in the progression without following it on paper.

Typical Ending

The "five" chord is not played during the last time through the progression (end of song). Instead, use the standard ending written below:

Fig. 2 Last four measures of a blues in "A."

Other Keys

Now try transposing the twelve-bar blues form to the keys of "E" and "C." Notice the I, IV, and V chords are still arranged the same, just moved to a new key center. Practice playing along with the examples below using open chords, barre chords, and power chord "boogie" patterns.

Blues in E

Fig. 3 66

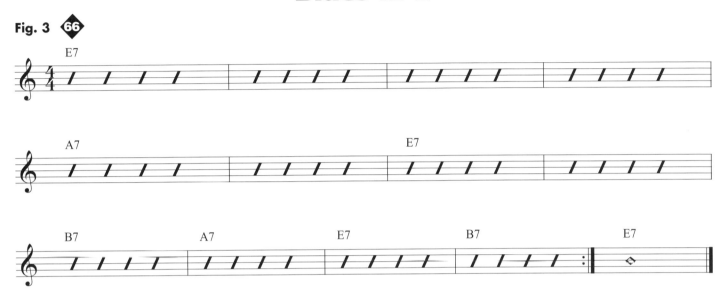

Blues in C

Fig. 4 67

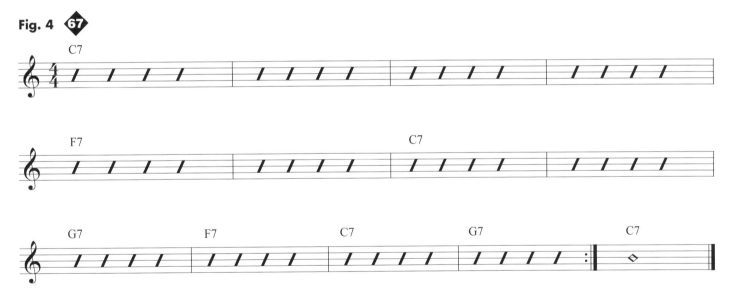

Substitute "Color" Chords

Certain musical styles are defined by the particular chord types used. For example, you already learned that rock relies heavily on power chords (and open chords) with distortion. So far in this chapter about blues music, you've exclusively used dominant seventh chords. However, two other chord types play an important part in the "sound" of the blues: the sixth and dominant ninth chords.

Let's take a look at the basic chord shapes:

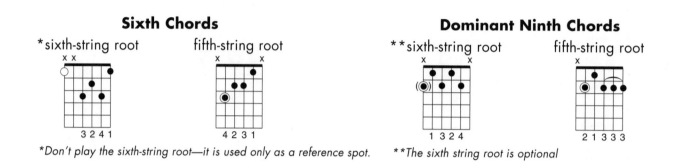

Sixth Chords

*sixth-string root   fifth-string root

3 2 4 1   4 2 3 1

*Don't play the sixth-string root—it is used only as a reference spot.

Dominant Ninth Chords

**sixth-string root   fifth-string root

1 3 2 4   2 1 3 3

**The sixth string root is optional

The dominant seventh, sixth, and dominant ninth chords can be exchanged for one another during a blues progression to add variety and flavor. Memorize the shapes and practice working them into your rhythm guitar playing. Below is an example of this concept in the key of A.

Fig. 5

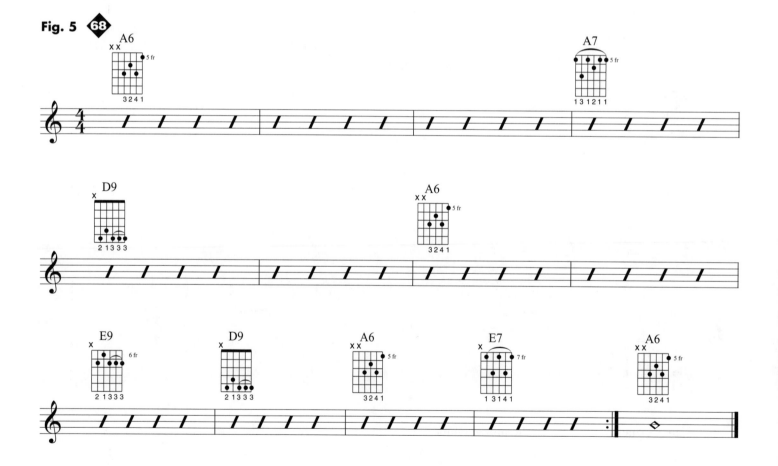

The Turnaround

The *turnaround* refers to the last two measures of the twelve-bar blues progression. The chord moves below are the most common turnaround variations. Listen to the CD and play along with each one. Then try moving them to other keys.

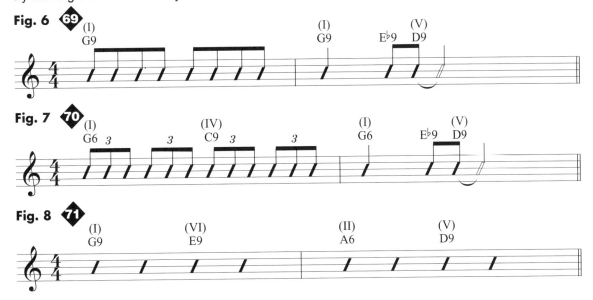

Blues Rhythm Patterns

Here are three more important blues rhythms that can be applied to either the I, IV, or V chords. The first two involve the *sliding sixth* chord and the third is an interpretation (via a "riff") of the dominant seventh chord. You can play any of these rhythm patterns when you see a dominant seventh on the chord chart.

Chapter Six

6 RYHTHM PLAYING

Three-String Triads

Guitarists often use smaller chord shapes as an effective rhythm tool. These three-string chord shapes, or inversions, are fragments of larger chords you already know. Take a look at the following three-string major triads:

◉ = root of triad
● = third or fifth of triad
○ = larger chord shape

#1
(root on top)

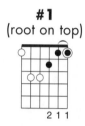

2 1 1

#2
(third on top)

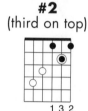

1 3 2

#3
(fifth on top)

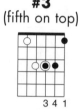

3 4 1

In the key of "A" major, the three shapes would appear across the neck as such:

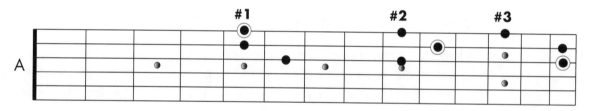

> NOTE: Each of the shapes above contain the notes of an A major triad in a different order. As a result, they are referred to as inversions. The most important note in the "partial" chords above is the top note. It has the greatest effect on how one chord connects to the next.

Chord Exercise

Write out the shapes for C major, D major, and G major:

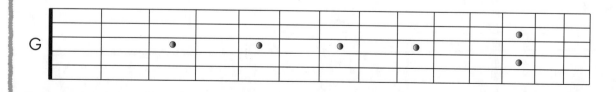

The Backbeat

Beats two and four (in 4/4 time) are known as the *backbeat*. Practice tapping your foot on every beat (1, 2, 3, 4) and striking chords on the backbeat (2 & 4). Experiment with different inversions of each chord to see how they connect. The CD plays each progression two times; once using a straight-eighth feel and again using a shuffle feel.

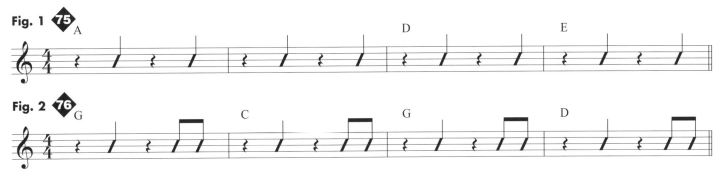

Minor Triad Inversions

Now convert the major triad "partials" from the previous page to minor. Study the new shapes below and compare the results. You'll notice only a one-note difference in each chord (the third chord tone is lowered one half step).

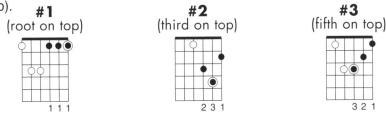

The three shapes of an A minor triad would appear across the neck as such:

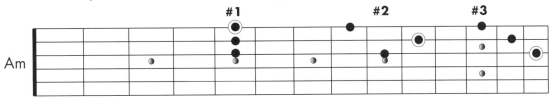

Chord Exercise

Write out the shapes for G minor, D minor, and E minor:

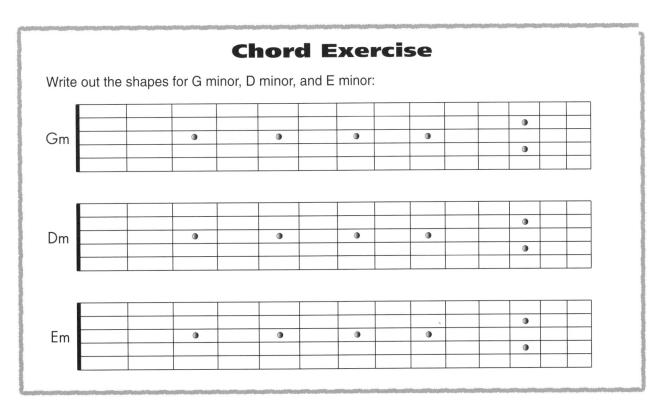

More Inversions

Two more common inversion shapes are located on strings 2-5.

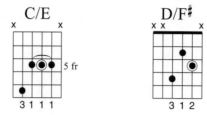

The "slash" chord symbol refers to the type of inversion. For example, "C/E" means a C triad with the E (third) in the bass. It is usually pronounced "C over E." However, guitarists often use these inversions even if the chord symbol does not call for it (Remember, the bass player should be playing lower notes than the guitar).

Try playing the examples below.

Fig. 3 77

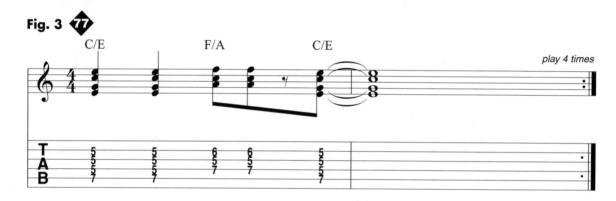

The next one uses added notes along with the original inversion shape.

Fig. 4 78

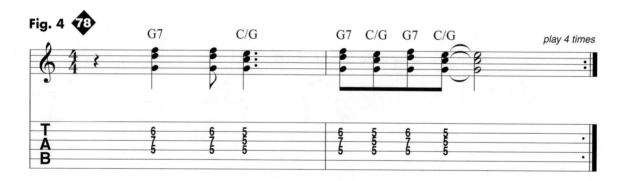

Progressions for Practice

Play along with the progressions below using as many strum and chord variations as possible. Try open chords, barre chords, power chords, three-string triads, and inversions. Work on one set of chord forms and introduce one new shape when you're ready. Remember, repetition is the key to improving your endurance and memorization skills.

"Suspended" and "Add" Chords

Most modern guitarists also use two other chord shapes called suspended and add (sometimes called "2" chords) chords. These chords expand the sound of the basic triad by adding an extra note. In fact, suspended and add chords are really just one-note variations on triad shapes you've already learned.

The Suspended Chord

As you already know, major triads are built from the first, third, and fifth (1-3-5) notes of the major scale. Suspended chords replace the third with the fourth, resulting in the formula 1-4-5. This is called "suspending the fourth," or in abbreviated terms "sus4" or simply "sus" chords. Since the third is not present, the chord is neither major or minor. In theory, suspended fourth chords should resolve to a major or minor chord. However, this is not always the case in modern music.

Memorize the shapes below and listen to their sound.

original major triad shape

1 3 4 2 1 1

sus4

3 4 1 1

original major triad shape

1 3 3 3

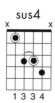

sus4

1 3 3 4

Another type of suspended chord replaces the third with the second, resulting in the formula (1-2-5).

sus2

1 3 4 1

sus2

1 3 4 1

The Add Chord

"Add" chords occur when notes are added to the basic triad shape. Most common is the add9. Practice the common add9 shapes below.

original major triad shape

1 3 4 2 1 1

add9

1 3 4 2 1 1

original major triad shape

3 2 1 1

add9

3 2 1 4

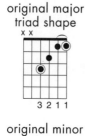

original major triad shape

1 3 3 3

add9

1 2 4 3

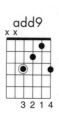

original minor triad shape

1 3 4 1 1 1

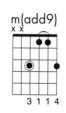

m(add9)

1 3 4 1 1 1

original minor triad shape

3 1 1 1

m(add9)

3 1 1 4

original minor triad shape

1 3 4 2

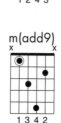

m(add9)

1 3 4 2

Progressions for Practice

Chapter Seven
SONGS AND PROGRESSIONS

7

Track #1

This progression is a basic rock groove with a straight-eight feel. Practice with the CD; then try it on your own at different tempos. Use eighth notes with all downstrokes, distortion, and slight palm muting. Strive for clock-like precision and a rock-solid attack on each chord.

Fig. 1 **87**

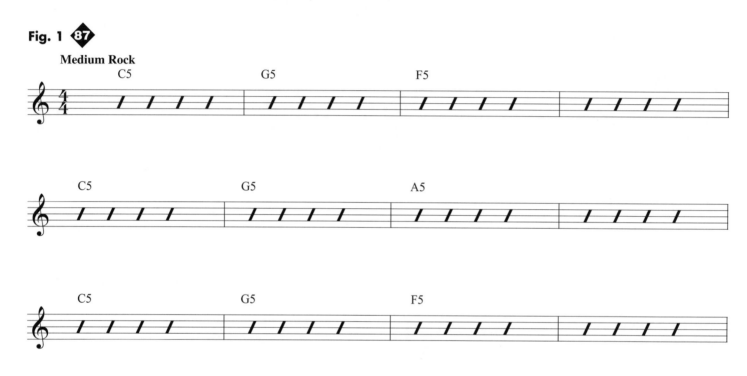

Track #2

Try using open position chords or moveable chords for this progression. The rhythm demonstrated in the figure below is generic to many styles. Concentrate on a steady groove and follow the suggested dynamics.

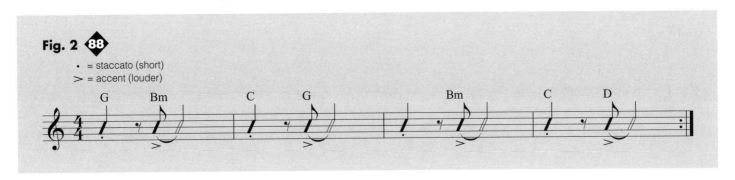

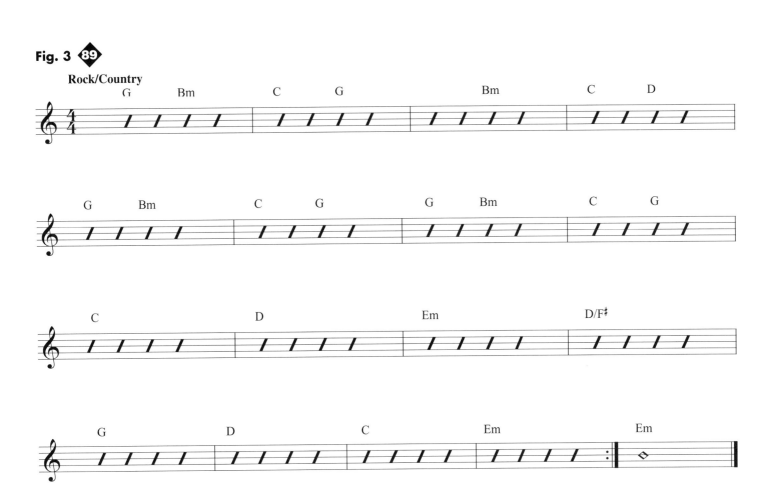

Track #3

This sample song features three definitive blues rhythm guitar styles in a sixteen-bar blues! Work on each part separately and then smooth out the transitions. Also, try substituting other voicings for the ones written for you.

Fig. 39 90

Track #4

Track #4 features a simple reggae groove using steady backbeat accents and a shuffle feel. Use three-string triads throughout. Play the upbeat eighth notes using a staccato attack to help the part "swing."

Fig. 5

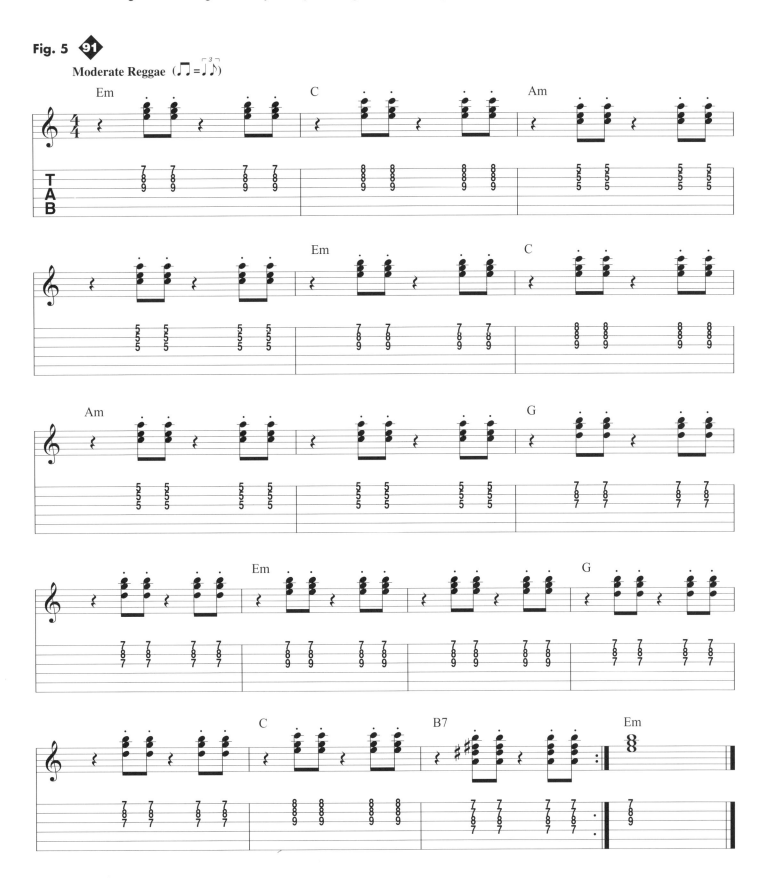

Review and Practice

It takes time to be able to play music in a convincing manner. Be patient, stay relaxed, and play everyday! Review Chapter 3 about practice tips and read through the additional practice ideas below. Good luck and have fun!

- Begin to "jam" and use your basic chord and scale shapes to improvise.

- Listen to records!

- Find transcriptions of your favorite songs and learn them.

- Find other players to "jam" with.

- Compose your own melodies and chord progressions.

- Test yourself on the names of the notes on the fretboard.

- Work with a metronome to improve your speed and technical ability... and conviction!

Audio Index

Musicians Institute Press

is the official series of Southern California's renowned music school, Musicians Institute. **MI** instructors, some of the finest musicians in the world, share their vast knowledge and experience with you – no matter what your current level. For guitar, bass, drums, vocals, and keyboards, **MI** Press offers the finest music curriculum for higher learning through a variety of series:

ESSENTIAL CONCEPTS
Designed from MI core curriculum programs.

MASTER CLASS
Designed from MI elective courses.

PRIVATE LESSONS
Tackle a variety of topics "one-on-one" with MI faculty instructors.

BASS

Arpeggios for Bass
by Dave Keif • Private Lessons
00695133 . . . . $12.95

The Art of Walking Bass
A Method for Acoustic or Electric Bass
by Bob Magnusson • Master Class
00695168 Book/CD Pack. $17.95

Bass Fretboard Basics
by Paul Farnen • Essential Concepts
00695201 . . . . $12.95

Bass Playing Techniques
by Alexis Sklarevski • Essential Concepts
00695207 . . . . $16.95

Grooves for Electric Bass
by David Keif • Private Lessons
00695265 Book/CD Pack. $14.95

Latin Bass
The Essential Guide to Afro-Cuban and Brazilian Styles
by George Lopez and David Keif • Private Lessons
00695543 Book/CD Pack. $14.95

Music Reading for Bass
by Wendy Wrehovcsik • Essential Concepts
00695203 . . . . $10.95

Odd-Meter Bassics
by Dino Monoxelos • Private Lessons
00695170 Book/CD Pack. $14.95

GUITAR

Advanced Scale Concepts & Licks for Guitar
by Jean Marc Belkadi • Private Lessons
00695298 Book/CD Pack $14.95

Advanced Guitar Soloing
By Daniel Gilbert & Beth Marlis • Essential Concepts
00695636 Book/CD Pack. $19.95

Basic Blues Guitar
by Steve Trovato • Private Lessons
00695180 Book/CD Pack $14.95

Classical & Fingerstyle Guitar Techniques
by David Oakes • Master Class
00695171 Book/CD Pack. $14.95

Contemporary Acoustic Guitar
by Eric Paschal & Steve Trovato • Master Class
00695320 Book/CD Pack. $16.95

Creative Chord Shapes
by Jamie Findlay • Private Lessons
00695172 Book/CD Pack. $9.95

Diminished Scale for Guitar
by Jean Marc Belkadi • Private Lessons
00695227 Book/CD Pack. $9.95

Essential Rhythm Guitar
Patterns, Progressions and Techniques for All Styles
by Steve Trovato • Private Lessons
00695181 Book/CD Pack. $14.95

Funk Guitar: The Essential Guide
by Ross Bolton • Private Lessons
00695419 Book/CD Pack. $14.95

Guitar Basics
by Bruce Buckingham • Private Lessons
00695134 Book/CD Pack. $16.95

Guitar Hanon
by Peter Deneff • Private Lessons
00695321 . . . . $9.95

Guitar Lick-tionary
By Dave Hill • Private Lessons
00695482 Book/CD Pack. $17.95

Guitar Soloing
by Dan Gilbert & Beth Marlis • Essential Concepts
00695190 Book/CD Pack. $19.95
00695638 Video $19.95

Harmonics for Guitar
by Jamie Findlay • Private Lessons
00695169 Book/CD Pack. $9.95

Jazz Guitar Chord System
by Scott Henderson • Private Lessons
00695291 . . . . $7.95

Jazz Guitar Improvisation
by Sid Jacobs • Master Class
00695128 Book/CD Pack. $17.95
00695639 Video $19.95

Jazz-Rock Triad Improvising
by Jean Marc Belkadi • Private Lessons
00695361 Book/CD Pack. $14.95

Latin Guitar
The Essential Guide to Brazilian and Afro-Cuban Rhythms
by Bruce Buckingham • Master Class
00695379 Book/CD Pack. $14.95

Modern Approach to Jazz, Rock & Fusion Guitar
by Jean Marc Belkadi • Private Lessons
00695143 Book/CD Pack. $14.95

Modes for Guitar
by Tom Kolb • Private Lessons
00695555 Book/CD Pack. $16.95

Music Reading for Guitar
by David Oakes • Essential Concepts
00695192 . . . . $16.95

The Musician's Guide to Recording Acoustic Guitar
by Dallan Beck • Private Lessons
00695505 Book/CD Pack. $12.95

Practice Trax for Guitar
by Danny Gill • Private Lessons
00695601 Book/CD Pack. $14.95

Rhythm Guitar
by Bruce Buckingham & Eric Paschal • Essential Concepts
00695188 Book. $16.95
00695644 Video $19.95

Rock Lead Basics
by Nick Nolan & Danny Gill • Master Class
00695144 Book/CD Pack. $15.95
00695637 Video $19.95

Rock Lead Performance
by Nick Nolan & Danny Gill • Master Class
00695278 Book/CD Pack. $16.95

Rock Lead Techniques
by Nick Nolan & Danny Gill • Master Class
00695146 Book/CD Pack. $15.95

Slap & Pop Technique For Guitar
00695645 Book/CD Pack. $12.95

Texas Blues Guitar
by Robert Calva • Private Lessons
00695340 Book/CD Pack. $16.95

FOR MORE INFORMATION, SEE YOUR LOCAL MUSIC DEALER,
OR WRITE TO:

HAL•LEONARD®
CORPORATION
7777 W. BLUEMOUND RD. P.O. BOX 13819 MILWAUKEE, WI 53213

Visit Hal Leonard Online at **www.halleonard.com**